HOMESTEADS

PHOTOGRAPHS BY PETER MAGUBANE

TEXT BY SANDRA KLOPPER

Published by Struik Publishers
(a division of New Holland Publishing (South Africa) (Pty) Ltd)

London • Cape Town • Sydney • Auckland

Garfield House   14 Aquatic Drive
86 Edgware Road   Frenchs Forest
W2 2EA London   NSW 2086
United Kingdom   Australia

80 McKenzie Street   218 Lake Road
Cape Town 8001   Northcote, Auckland
South Africa   New Zealand

Website: www.struik.co.za

ISBN 1 86872 517 0

Design director Janice Evans
Publishing manager Annlerie van Rooyen
Design Illana Fridkin
Managing editor Lesley Hay-Whitton
Proofreader Glynne Newlands
French translator Jean-Paul Houssière
German translator Friedel Herrmann

Reproduction by Hirt & Carter (Cape) Pty Ltd
Printed and bound by APP Printers, Singapore

Front cover: Ndebele wall painting.
Back cover: Dwelling at the Sotho cultural village
near Golden Gate in the Free State.
Page 1: Married Ndebele woman.
Page 2 (left): Venda homestead.
Page 2 (right): Interior of a South Sotho homestead.
Page 3 (left): South Sotho wall decoration.
Page 3 (right): Children playing with wheelbarrow.
Opposite: Tswana homestead.
Page 6: Married Bantwane women seated in the
shade of a homestead.

INTRODUCTION

South African rural communities continue to build their homesteads from mud bricks and readily available materials like wood, stone and thatching grass. Where possible, these materials are supplemented with corrugated iron sheeting and steel frame windows, but items of this kind are not always easy to obtain in outlying areas. In many cases, commercially manufactured materials are either too expensive or too difficult to transport on the often badly maintained roads servicing relatively inaccessible areas. Rural communities devote much time to maintaining their homes, which are highly susceptible to damage by heavy rains and various insects, notably termites. The latter threat can be obviated by using stone and the wood of the tamboti tree (*Spirostachys africana*), known to repel insects, but not all communities have access to these durable indigenous materials. In many rural areas men still tend to leave home to work in the cities, returning only at Christmas and Easter. It is therefore mainly women who bear the burden of responsibility for looking after rural homesteads. In some places, these women continue to decorate their homes with bold geometric designs using either clay or commercially available paints. Alternatively, they etch delicate patterns into the wet surface of newly plastered walls. Generally speaking these motifs are based on traditional designs, like those associated with certain beadwork styles. But these comparatively old patterns are now often interspersed with images derived from magazines and the logos of well-known companies like Nike. In the case of Ndebele murals, there has also been a tendency to allude to the access urban dwellers have to electricity and running water, and to other marvels of modern life, like aeroplanes and the spacious double-storey domestic dwellings found in large cities like Johannesburg and Pretoria. These murals, which appear most often on the exterior walls of homesteads and in courtyard areas, are usually repainted yearly either before or after the summer rains. Unlike those found in some interior spaces, their production is generally informed by a desire to elicit the admiration and respect of neighbours and passers-by. As such, murals play an important role not only in providing an outlet for the expression of female creativity, but also in reinforcing the sense of cohesion valued by most rural communities.

INTRODUCTION

Dans toute l'Afrique du Sud, les communautés rurales continuent de construire leurs maisons en briques de boue séchée et d'autres matériaux, comme le bois, la pierre et le chaume qui sont faciles à obtenir. Si disponibles, on utilise aussi de la tôle ondulée et des fenêtres à châssis métallique, bien que de tels matériaux ne soient pas toujours faciles à obtenir dans les endroits reculés. Bien souvent aussi, ces matériaux sont soit trop chers, ou trop difficiles à livrer dans les endroits reculés à cause du mauvais état des routes. Les communautés rurales consacrent un temps considérable à l'entretien de leurs homes, ceux-ci se détériorant constamment à cause des éléments peu cléments et la destruction par de nombreux insectes, notamment les termites. Bien qu'il soit possible de renforcer la construction par l'utilisation de pierres et du bois de tamboti (*Spirostachys africana*) dont l'odeur chasse les insectes, ces matériaux indigènes ne sont pas toujours disponibles partout. Dans de nombreuses communautés rurales, les hommes vont travailler à la ville, ne revenant chez eux qu'à Pâques et à la Noël; la responsabilité de s'occuper de la propriété sera donc celle des femmes. Dans certains endroits, les femmes décorent leurs maisons avec des motifs géométriques très voyants, utilisant soit de l'argile ou de la peinture. Parfois aussi, elles gravent des motifs délicats sur la surface encore humide de murs fraîchement recouverts. En général ces motifs sont basés sur les styles traditionnels, semblables à ceux que l'on trouve sur les objets perlés. Toutefois ces styles relativement anciens sont souvent ravivés par des images inspirées de magazines et d'emblèmes de marques bien connues, comme Nike. Dans les peintures murales des Ndebeles, par exemple, il y a une tendance à faire allusion aux conforts de la vie moderne, comme l'eau courante et l'électricité. Ces peintures qui décorent le plus souvent les murs de clôture et l'extérieur des maisons, sont généralement refaites chaque année, soit avant, ou après la saison des pluies. Contrairement aux décorations intérieures, celles des murs externes visent à provoquer l'admiration et le respect des voisins et passants. En tant que telles, les peintures murales sont importantes, car elles permettent de donner libre cours à l'imagination, et de renforcer le sens communautaire spécialement prisé par les habitants de la campagne.

EINFÜHRUNG

Überall in Südafrika benutzt die ländliche Bevölkerung weiterhin selbstgefertigte, ungebrannte Lehmziegel und andere verfügbare Materialien, wie Holz, Steine und Reet, zum Bau ihrer Heimstätten. Wenn möglich, werden solche Baustoffe mit Wellblech und stählernen Fensterrahmen ergänzt, aber diese sind in den abgelegenen Gebieten nicht immer erhältlich. Fernerhin sind Handelswaren oftmals zu kostspielig oder zu schwer transportierbar auf den schlechten Straßen, die durch die unwirtlichen Gebiete führen. Die Bevölkerung auf dem Land verwendet viel Zeit darauf, ihre Heimstätten instand zu halten, denn diese sind sehr anfällig für Regenschäden und Insektenbefall, besonders durch Termiten. Gegen letztere schützt man sich, indem Steine und das stark riechende, insektenabweisende Holz des Tambotibaumes (*Spirostachys africana*) verwendet werden, aber diese Baumaterialien kommen nicht überall vor. In vielen Landgebieten ziehen die Männer in die Städte, wo sie Arbeit finden, und kehren nur zu Ostern und Weihnachten heim. Daher fällt die Hauptlast bei der Instandhaltung der Heimstätten mehrheitlich auf die Frauen. In manchen Gegenden dekorieren diese Frauen weiterhin das Heim mit auffälligen geometrischen Mustern und benutzen dazu entweder Lehm oder handelsübliche Farben. Manchmal versehen sie auch die noch feuchten, frisch verputzten Wände mit zierlichen Dessins. Vorwiegend entsprechen die Motive traditionellen Mustern, wie sie auch in den Perlenarbeiten zu sehen sind. Aber diese relativ alten Muster sind heutzutage oft durchsetzt mit Wiedergaben von Bildern aus Zeitschriften oder dem Logo bekannter Firmen, wie Nike. Was die Wandgemälde der Ndebele anbetrifft, findet man auch Hinweise auf Annehmlichkeiten der Stadtbewohner, etwa Strom und fließend Wasser, und Errungenschaften des modernen Lebens, wie Flugzeuge und Hochhäuser, die in großen Städten wie Johannesburg und Pretoria angetroffen werden. Wandmalereien auf den Außenwänden der Häuser oder in Innenhöfen werden gewöhnlich alljährlich nach der Regenzeit erneuert. Im Gegensatz zu Innendekorationen, zielen Außendekorationen darauf ab, Bewunderung und Respekt bei Nachbarn und Vorübergehenden zu finden. Als solches sind sie nicht nur Ausdruck weiblicher Kreativität, sondern auch eine Bestätigung der Zugehörigkeit, auf den die ländliche Bevölkerung Wert legt.

South Sotho women create bold optical effects in their mural designs. While many of these designs may seem abstract, most are inspired by natural forms, notably flowers and the leaves of plants like maize, which the women grow to feed their families.

Les femmes south sotho décorent leurs murs avec des motifs très voyants. Bien que paraissant abstraits, la plupart de ces motifs sont inspirés par la nature, notamment les fleurs et les feuilles de plantes comme le maïs, que les femmes cultivent.

Die Frauen der Süd-Sotho erzielen starke, optische Effekte in ihren Wandmalereien. Viele der Muster mögen abstrakt wirken, aber sie sind durch natürliche Formen inspiriert, besonders Blumen und Blätter von Pflanzen wie Mais, der überall angepflanzt wird.

Although some South Sotho murals are characterized by stark juxtapositions of commercially manufactured paints, others rely on the use of comparatively neutral earth tones. It was only once brightly coloured paints became readily available in the course of the 20th century that women sometimes abandoned the practice of using locally available natural pigments.

Bien que certaines décorations south sotho soient caractérisées par leurs couleurs bariolées, d'autres sont bien moins criardes, de ton plus neutre. Une fois que la peinture devint disponible en commerce dans le courant du 20ième siècle, les femmes abandonnaient de temps en temps l'usage de pigments naturels pour utiliser des couleurs vives.

Obwohl einige der Wandmalereien der Süd-Sotho durch grelle Farbkombinationen mit handelsüblichen Farben auffallen, sind andere wiederum in erdigen, neutralen Tönen gehalten. Die Verwendung natürlicher Pigmentstoffe nahm erst ab, als im Laufe des 20. Jahrhunderts die leuchtenden synthetischen Farben allgemein erhältlich wurden.

The Ndzundza Ndebele were the first to use commercially manufactured paints. Their decision to do so as early as the 1940s was motivated by a desire to proclaim their difference from other South African groups living in present-day Mpumalanga.

Les Ndzundza Ndebeles furent les premiers à utiliser la peinture manufacturée. Cette tendance commença durant les années 40, et fut motivée par le désir de se différencier des autres communautés sud africaines vivant dans le Mpumalanga.

Die Ndzundza-Ndebele waren die ersten, die handelsübliche Farben benutzten. Sie entschieden sich schon in den 1940er Jahren dafür, getrieben von dem Verlangen, sich von anderen südafrikanischen Volksgruppen im heutigen Mpumalanga zu unterscheiden.

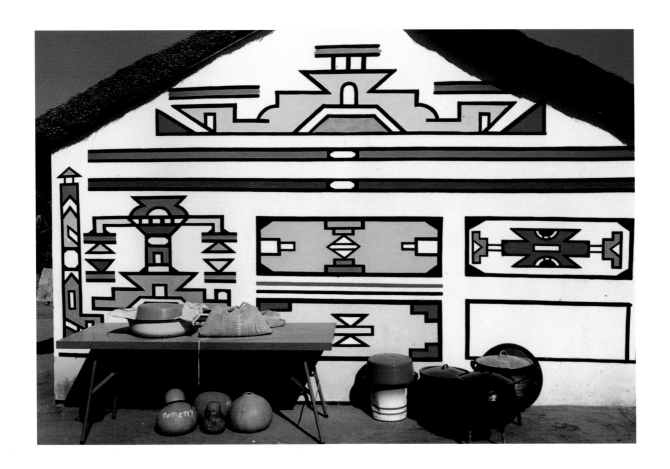

Unlike other ethnic groups, the Ndebele, indentured following a bloody encounter with white farmers in 1883, failed to secure communal lands through the Land Act of 1936. Their highly visible murals served to register their protest at this exclusion.

En 1883, suite à des démêlés sanglants avec des fermiers blancs, les Ndebeles furent employés sous contrat, mais n'obtinrent pas de terres suivant la loi de 1936. Leurs décors muraux très distincts servaient à marquer leurs protestations contre cette exclusion.

Da sie nach den Kämpfen von 1883 zwangsverpflichtet und verstreut wurden, erhielten die Ndebele kein kommunales Land, als das Landgesetz von 1936 in Kraft trat. Die auffälligen Wandbemalungen waren Ausdruck ihres Protestes gegen diese Ausgrenzung.

In some cases, Ndebele murals underline the importance people attach to traditional practices. Their commitment to these practices is reflected in images depicting older forms of dress, like beaded blankets, and the carrying of shields and fighting sticks by male initiates.

Certaines des peintures murales ndebeles soulignent l'importance attachée aux pratiques traditionnelles. Les images illustrent les anciens styles de costumes, comme les couvertures ornées de perles, et le port de boucliers et de bâtons de combat par les initiés.

Mitunter betonen die Wandmalereien der Ndebele den hohen Stellenwert der Bräuche. Wie sehr sie sich diesen Bräuchen noch verpflichtet fühlen, zeigen Bilder, auf denen die alte Volkstracht, wie perlenbestickte Decken, und das Tragen von Schilden und Kampfstöcken männlicher Initianden zu sehen sind.

Many Ndebele women still combine older mural designs with the more colourful, densely patterned styles adopted in the 1940s. By doing so, they pay homage to the achievements of their mothers and grandmothers while affirming their own creativity.

De nombreuses Ndebeles entremêlent toujours les anciens motifs avec ceux plus denses et plus vibrants introduits dans les années '40. Ce faisant, elles rendent hommage à la vaillance de leurs mères et grands-mères, tout en démontrant leur propre créativité.

Viele Ndebele-Frauen verbinden die alten Motive der Wandbemalung mit den bunten, stark gemusterten Stilen, die in den 1940er Jahren aufkamen. Damit erkennen sie die Leistungen ihrer Mütter und Großmütter an und betonen gleichzeitig eigene Kreativität.

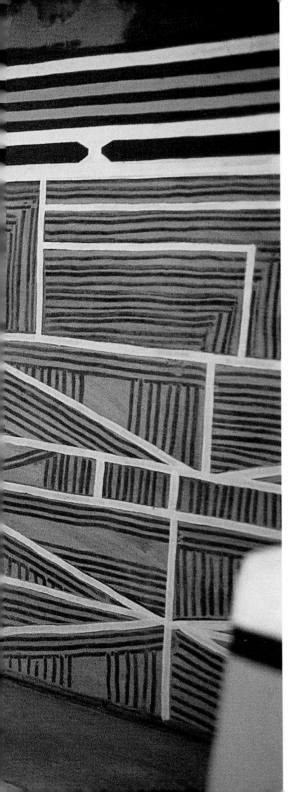

Both contemporary and older Ndebele murals are characterized by a bold sense of design. Their impact depends partly on the stark bands of white and, in some cases, also black pigments used to isolate and define the individual geometric patterns.

Les peintures murales ndebeles, anciennes et modernes, sont typiques par leur style démonstratif. L'impression créée dépend en partie du contraste entre les bandes noires et blanches, et, dans certains cas, de l'usage de pigments noirs pour isoler des formes géométriques particulières.

Sowohl die neuzeitlichen als auch die älteren Wandmalereien der Ndebele zeigen eine starke Stilprägung. Der Eindruck beruht teilweise auf den breiten, weißen Linien und andererseits auch auf den schwarzen Pigmenten, die individuelle geometrische Muster voneinander abheben und betonen.

South Sotho women sometimes etch patterns into the wet earth of newly plastered walls. Since the visual impact of these designs depends in part on the way light falls on the surface of the walls, the appearance of murals of this kind changes in the course of a single day. Today some Zulu-speaking communities decorate their circular homesteads in emulation of the etched designs found on the homes of neighbouring Sotho communities.

Parfois, les femmes south sotho gravent des motifs dans la surface encore humide de murs fraîchement recouverts. L'impression donnée par ces motifs dépendant de la direction de la lumière, l'apparence du mur change d'heure en heure. De nos jours, certaines communautés zouloues décorent leurs huttes circulaires, s'inspirant des gravures murales de leurs voisins sothos.

Die Frauen der Süd-Sotho ritzen manchmal Muster in die noch feuchten, frisch verputzten Wände. Da der visuelle Eindruck dieser Motive teilweise davon abhängig ist, wie das Licht auf die Wandfläche fällt, verändert sich der Eindruck solcher Malereien im Laufe eines einzigen Tages. Einige der zulusprachigen Gruppen verzieren heutzutage ihre Rundhütten in Nachahmung der eingeritzten Motive ihrer Sotho-Nachbarn.

Occasionally, South Sotho women create murals by embedding pebbles (*opposite*) into the newly plastered walls instead of scratching into the wet plaster (*below*). The production of pebble mosaic is comparatively labour intensive.

Parfois les femmes south sotho décorent leurs murs en incrustant des cailloux dans la surface alors qu'elle est encore humide (*ci-contre*) au lieu d'y graver des motifs (*ci-dessous*). La création de ces mosaïques exige une main d'œuvre importante comparé aux gravures.

Frauen der Süd-Sotho fertigen auch Wandbilder an, indem sie Kieselsteine (*gegenüber*) in die frisch verputzten Wände drücken, statt die Muster einzuritzen (*unten*). Diese Mosaikmuster sind arbeitsintensiv wegen des Zeitaufwandes beim Sammeln der Steine.

Although Tsonga murals rely on the use of earth tones, they are unusually bold, and can therefore be seen from a considerable distance. In some cases, contemporary Tsonga designs emulate the hearts, diamonds, spades and clover-leaf motifs found on playing cards (*see also* pages 28-29).

Le style des peintures murales tsongas, bien que principalement de ton neutre, est visible de loin grâce à ses motifs hardis. Parfois on sait reconnaître dans les motifs tsongas contemporains les cœurs, carreaux, trèfles et piques des cartes à jouer (*voir aussi* pages 28-29).

Obwohl bei den Wandmalereien der Tsonga die Erdfarben dominieren, sind sie außergewöhnlich auffällig gemustert und daher weithin sichtbar. Manchmal erinnern die Motive an Spielkarten, und man kann Herz, Pik, Kreuz und Karo erkennen (*siehe auch* Seiten 28-29).

In common with Tsonga women, Pedi women use natural earth tones. Like some other South African groups they use designs to accentuate the corners and doorways of courtyard areas. The need to repaint walls stained by water dripping from roof tops during the rainy season is obviated by adding similar bands of colour to the lower sections of their homes.

Comme les Tsongas, les femmes pedis utilisent les tons naturels et rustiques de la terre. En commun avec d'autres groupes sud africains, elles mettent en évidence les coins et embrasures de portes par des motifs choisis. On évite la repeinte des murs décolorés par la pluie, en ajoutant des bandes de même couleur au bas des habitations.

Genau wie die Tsonga-Frauen benutzen die Frauen der Pedi Erdfarben. Wie andere Völker in Südafrika betonen sie gerne die Ecken und Türeingänge der Innenhöfe mit Malereien. In der Regenzeit verursacht vom Dach abtropfendes Wasser oft Flecken an den Wänden. Um ein Überstreichen zu umgehen, werden ähnliche Farben auf den unteren Teilen der Hauswände verwandt.

Despite the widespread practice of producing murals, homesteads are often left unadorned. There are various reasons for this but, in most cases, women are simply too busy attending to their fields and families to devote time to activities of this kind.

Même si la coutume de décorer les murs est répandue, il n'en est pas toujours ainsi. Il y a plusieurs raisons pour cela, mais dans la plupart des cas, les femmes sont trop occupées par leurs activités domestiques pour s'appliquer à la décoration.

Das Bemalen der Hauswände ist zwar weit verbreitet, aber es ist keineswegs ungewöhnlich, daß einige Frauen es nicht machen. Hierfür gibt es verschiedene Gründe, wobei der wichtigste wohl ist, daß die Frauen einfach zu beschäftigt sind, sich um die Felder und die Familie zu kümmern und nicht die Zeit für dieserart Tätigkeit finden.

People tend to rely on unfired mud bricks to build their homes (*see* pages 34-35). Other locally available materials like reeds and saplings are less common, mainly because these are prone to being attacked by wood-boring insects, but materials like these are often used for storage areas (*above*).

La plupart des communautés sud africaines préfèrent utiliser des briques de boue séchée pour construire leurs maisons (*voir* pages 34-35). L'usage de matériaux trouvés sur place, comme les roseaux et les arbrisseaux, est moins répandu, parce qu'ils attirent les insectes.

Die Mehrheit der Volksgruppen in Südafrika verwendet ungebrannte Lehmziegel zum Häuserbau (*siehe* Seiten 34-35). Die in der Umgebung vorhandenen Baumaterialien, wie Schilf und junge Baumstämme, werden weniger benutzt, weil sie für Holzschädlinge anfällig sind.

Like women from other South African communities, Ndebele muralists often highlight the doorways of homesteads with bold mural designs. In most cases, the production of visual markers of this kind is motivated by aesthetic rather than symbolic considerations.

Comme les femmes des autres communautés sud africaines, les artistes ndebeles enjolivent les embrasures de portes avec des motifs très voyants. Leur style est motivé plus par l'esthétique que par raison symbolique.

Ebenso wie Frauen anderer südafrikanischer Volksgruppen betonen die Ndebele-Frauen mehrheitlich die Türeingänge mit auffälligen Bemalungen. Meistens wird diese optische Markierung aus ästhetischen Gründen angebracht und ist nicht irgendwie symbolträchtig.

The practice of accentuating doorways with mural details may also be ascribed to their association with the homestead's ancestors. In addition, these and other decorative features also serve to underline the pride women take in looking after their homes.

La pratique de mettre en évidence les embrasures de porte avec des motifs minutieux, démontre également leur association avec les ancêtres, anciens occupants de la maison. De plus, ces décorations plus spéciales servent à démontrer le soin que prennent les femmes pour leurs habitations.

Der Brauch, die Eingangstüren durch Wandmalereien hervorzuheben, kann auch mit der Bedeutung den gerade Türeingänge für die Ahnen haben, in Verbindung gebracht werden. Fernerhin unterstreichen diese und andere Dekorationen auch den Stolz der Hausfrau auf ihr Heim.

South Sotho women decorate the surrounds of doorways and windows with a range of motifs. While some of these are drawn from nature, others are inspired by the profiles of dressing tables and similar commercially manufactured items of furniture.

Les femmes south sotho décorent les embrasures des portes et des fenêtres avec divers motifs. Bien que certains de ceux-ci soient inspirés par la nature, d'autres viennent d'objets plus communs, comme les tables et autres meubles trouvés en magasin.

Die Frauen der Süd-Sotho umranden ihre Türen und Fenster mit sehr unterschiedlichen Mustern. Einige sind der Natur entlehnt, während andere die geschwungene Form von Frisiertoiletten und ähnlichen Möbelstücken nachahmen.

While the practice of highlighting the surroundings of windows and doorways is very common throughout South Africa, these features are usually accentuated through simple colour contrasts rather than the use of patterns. The tendency to raise the thresholds of doors is motivated not by decorative considerations, but rather by the need to prevent the homestead from flooding.

Alors que la pratique de mettre en valeur l'encadrement des portes et des fenêtres est très répandue, l'effet voulu est atteint par un simple jeu de contraste de couleurs plutôt que par l'utilisation de motifs. L'usage de surélever le seuil des portes n'est pas motivé par des raisons esthétiques, mais pour empêcher l'eau d'entrer en cas d'inondation.

Auch wenn der Brauch, Fenster und Türen farblich zu umrahmen, in ganz Südafrika weit verbreitet ist, geschieht dies meistens mittels Kontrastfarben und nicht durch aufgemalte Muster. Daß die Türeingänge erhöht sind, hat keinen dekorativen Grund, sondern soll eine Überschwemmung der Häuser verhindern.

Women from Tswana and South Sotho communities often use relief plasterwork to accentuate doorways, windows and other details like the outer perimeters of the homestead's façades. The contrast between these surrounds and the rest of the façade is usually enhanced by unpainted relief work.

Les femmes des communautés tswanas et south sotho accentuent souvent les portes, fenêtres et autres détails de façade, ainsi que les murs de clôture, avec des motifs en relief. En ne les peignant pas, on augmente le contraste, ce qui les fait ressortir contre le fond.

Bei den Tswana und Süd-Sotho umranden die Frauen Türen, Fenster und andere Blickpunkte der äußeren Fassaden ihrer Heimstätten oft mit Reliefputz. Um den Kontrast solcher Umrandung noch hervorzuheben, wird dieser Reliefputz gewöhnlich nicht angestrichen.

While the use of mural details is more commonly found on the exterior of buildings, women also take considerable pride in decorating the interior of their homes. Colourful details may be found in communal spaces like kitchens, but some women decorate private spaces like bedrooms as well.

Les South Sotho aiment construire des étagères et des buffets avec des matériaux comme l'argile. De nos jours, ces constructions encastrées sont souvent ornées de pages découpées dans des magazines, mais dans le passé, quand ces images étaient plus difficiles à obtenir, les femmes découpaient de minutieux motifs dans du papier journal.

Wanddekorationen werden zwar gewöhnlich an der Außenseite der Baulichkeiten angebracht, aber die Frauen setzen auch besonderen Stolz darein, das Innere ihres Heimes zu schmücken. Die allgemeinen Wohnräume wie etwa die Küchen werden häufig mit farbenfreudigen Dekorationen versehen, aber manche Frauen verzieren auch noch Privatsphären wie die Schlafräume.

While the top of a stove may serve as a shelf, the South Sotho build display shelves and sideboards from materials like clay. These built-in structures are often decorated with the pages of advertisements but in the past, when colourful images of this kind were comparatively rare, women usually cut delicate motifs into black and white newsprint.

Alors que le dessus d'une cuisinière pourra servir d'étagère, les South Sothos construisent des étagères et des buffets avec des matériaux comme l'argile. Ces constructions encastrées sont souvent ornées de réclames, mais dans le passé, quand ces images bariolées étaient difficiles à obtenir, les femmes découpaient de minutieux motifs dans du papier journal.

Das Oberteil des Herdes wird als Abstellfläche genutzt, aber die Süd-Sotho konstruieren auch Anrichten und Simse aus Lehm. Diese eingebauten Strukturen verziert man heutzutage oft mit Reklamebildern aus Glanzpapier, aber früher, als solche Bilder noch nicht oder nur selten zur Verfügung standen, fertigten die Frauen Scherenschnitte in schwarzweiß aus Zeitungspapier an.

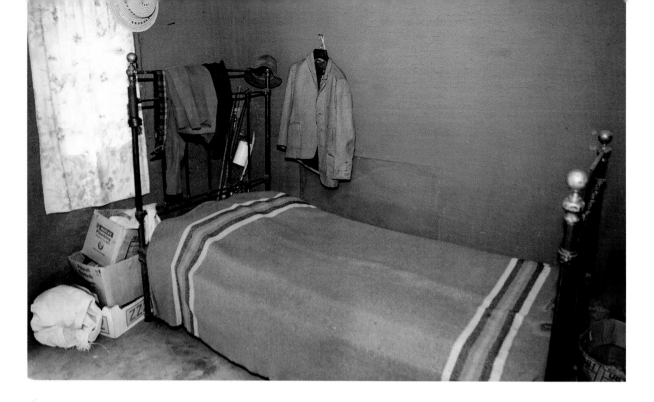

In the past, rural people seldom had access to cupboards. Clothing was stored in boxes, and jackets were hung from nails in the walls and rafters (*see* pages 50-51). Old brass beds also afforded knobs and crossbars for hats and other personal effects.

Dans le passé, les habitations rurales contenaient rarement des armoires. Les effets étaient rangés dans des cartons, les vestes pendues aux murs (*voir* pages 50-51). Les anciens lits de cuivre avaient des ornements auxquels on pouvait accrocher chapeaux et autres effets.

Schränke gab es bei der Landbevölkerung früher kaum. Bekleidung wurde in Kartons aufbewahrt, Jacketts hingen an Wandnägeln oder Balken (*siehe* Seiten 50-51). Die alten Bettgestelle boten Knäufe und Stangen für Hüte und andere persönliche Dinge.

Ndebele women sometimes decorate bedroom areas with intensely coloured murals similar to those found on the exterior walls of their homes. Other decorative accents are afforded by carefully arranged blankets and beadwork items.

Les femmes ndebeles décorent parfois les murs de leurs chambres à coucher avec des couleurs flamboyantes, semblables à celles utilisées à l'extérieur. Elles garnissent aussi la pièce avec des couvertures et ornements perlés sélectionnés judicieusement.

Auch in den Schlafräumen dekorieren die Ndebele-Frauen die Wände manchmal mit sehr farbenfreudigen Malereien, ähnlich wie auf den Außenwänden. Weitere dekorative Effekte werden durch sorgfältig drapierte Decken und ausgelegte Perlenarbeiten erzielt.

Some commercial blanket manufacturers produce designs aimed at particular groups, but Bantwane and other women sometimes decorate their rooms with blankets covered in motifs that seem out of keeping with the values of rural traditionalists.

Certains fabricants de couvertures offrent un choix de motifs destinés pour certains groupes, mais les Bantwanes décorent parfois leurs maisons avec des couvertures dont les motifs ne correspondent pas avec les valeurs des traditionalistes ruraux.

Einige Hersteller liefern Decken, deren Muster bestimmte Volksgruppen ansprechen, aber die Bantwane und andere Frauen schmücken ihre Räume manchmal mit Decken, deren Motive nicht mit den Vorgaben der ländlichen Traditionalisten übereinstimmen.

Venda women do not necessarily paint murals on homestead walls (*above*). But Venda artist Noria Mabasa, who displays her clay sculptures and woodcarvings in the courtyard of her home, also has large altar-like murals on the interior walls of her homestead.

Les femmes vendas ne peignent pas toujours les murs de leurs habitations (*ci-dessus*). L'artiste venda Noria Mabasa, qui expose ses sculptures en argile et en bois dans la cour de sa maison, a aussi de grandes peintures murales, comme des autels, à l'intérieur.

Die Wände der Heimstätten werden bei den Venda nicht unbedingt bemalt (*oben*). Aber die Künstlerin Noria Mabasa, die ihre Lehmskulpturen und Holzschnitzereien im Innenhof ausstellt, hat auch große, altarartige Wandmalereien auf den Innenwänden ihres Heimes.

Some Swazi (*right*) and Zulu-speaking groups still build thatched beehive structures. The thatch is usually stretched over a framework of pliable saplings once this framework has been embedded firmly into the ground. Alternatively, the thatch is built over a low mud brick wall. The advantage of the latter building method is that it generally requires comparatively little maintenance.

Certaines communautés swazies (*à droite*) et zouloues construisent encore des huttes en chaume. Celui-ci est attaché sur une structure faite de branches souples, ancrée solidement dans le sol. Parfois la hutte consiste en un mur bas en briques de boue séchée, également recouvert de chaume. Cette dernière méthode a l'avantage de ne pas exiger beaucoup d'entretien.

In einigen Gemeinden der Swasi (*rechts*) und Zulu baut man noch immer bienenkorbförmigen Rundhütten aus Schilf. Das Reet wird gewöhnlich über einen Rahmen aus biegsamen Zweigen befestigt, die man zuvor fest im Boden verankert hat. Oder das Reetgebilde wird auf einer niedrigen Mauer von Lehmziegeln angebracht, was den Vorteil geringer Instandhaltung mit sich bringt.

Unlike men, who tend to work in urban areas, women still look after rural homesteads. Partly for this reason they are often solely responsible for all domestic chores, including the collection of cow dung (used as fuel), washing clothes and the grinding of maize.

Alors que les hommes travaillent à la ville, les femmes à la campagne s'occupent des habitations. Leurs responsabilités comprennent toutes les corvées domestiques, y compris le ramassage de bouse sèche qui sert de combustible, la lessive et la mouture du maïs.

Im Gegensatz zu den Männern, die in den Stadtgebieten zur Arbeit gehen, versorgen die Frauen auf dem Land immer noch die Heimstätten. Dadurch tragen sie die alleinige Verantwortung für alle häuslichen Arbeiten, wozu Wäsche waschen, das Zermahlen von Mais und Einsammeln von Kuhdung (der allgemein als Brennstoff verwendet wird) zählt.

Despite recent attempts to supply communities with water from bore holes close to their homes, many rural homesteads still lack easy access to this amenity. Women have to walk long distances to collect water, which they usually carry on their heads.

De nombreuses communautés ne possèdent pas encore de puits d'eau à proximité des habitations. Les femmes doivent alors aller chercher au loin l'eau dont elles ont besoin quotidiennement; celle ci est habituellement portée en équilibre sur la tête.

Trotz Bemühungen, Bohrlöcher in Siedlungsnähe anzulegen, mangelt es vielen ländlichen Heimstätten noch am Zugang zu dieser Annehmlichkeit. Frauen müssen zum Wasserholen lange Strecken zurücklegen. Die Behälter werden gewöhnlich auf dem Kopf getragen.

Rural women perform strenuous physical activities, including collecting materials to build or maintain homesteads. Thatching grass and reeds are used in the construction not only of roofs, but also of grain stores and other enclosures.

Les femmes doivent faire de lourdes corvées, comprenant le ramassage de matériaux pour l'entretien de l'habitation. Le chaume et les roseaux sont utilisés non seulement pour la construction des toits, mais aussi de réserves de grain et autres enclos.

Landfrauen verrichten schwere körperliche Arbeit, wie das Beschaffen der Baumaterialien zum Neubau oder zur Instandhaltung der Heimstätten. Reet und Schilf werden nicht nur zum Dachdecken verwendet, sondern auch für Getreidespeicher und Einfriedungen.

Most rural women around South Africa are involved in everyday tasks such as cooking, attending to the needs of children and sweeping the courtyards of their homes. Some of them nevertheless manage to devote time to adorning the walls and floors of homestead courtyards with designs that underline their pride in their role as homemakers. Important rituals associated with initiation and involving the use of salt and blood (*right*) also take place in these courtyards.

Les tâches ménagères des femmes de la campagne sont simples: elles préparent les repas, balayent la maison, s'occupent de leurs enfants. Néanmoins, certaines trouvent le temps de se consacrer à d'importants rituels et à décorer les murs et sol de leur habitation de motifs appliqués avec minutie, démontrant ainsi leurs qualités de femmes d'intérieur.

Die täglich anfallenden Hausarbeiten wie Kochen, Versorgung der Kinder und Fegen der Innenhöfe füllt die Zeit der meisten Landfrauen aus. Einige jedoch schaffen es außerdem noch, wichtige Riten zu zelebrieren und die Wände und Böden ihrer Heimstätten mit sorgfältig ausgeführten Dekorationen zu versehen, die unverkennbar ihren Stolz als Schöpferin eines Heimes unterstreichen.

Like most activities in rural communities, cooking is performed by women. During important celebrations maize porridge, steamed breads and pot-roasted meat obtained from ritually slaughtered animals are prepared in the open in large iron pots over wood-burning fires.

Comme la plupart des activités dans les communautés rurales, la préparation des repas est le travail des femmes. Lors de célébrations importantes, le maïs, le porridge, le pain et la viande venant d'animaux sacrifiés, sont préparés à l'extérieur dans de grands pots de fer, sur des feux de bois.

Wie fast alle anfallenden Arbeiten auf dem Lande ist auch das Kochen Frauensache. Bei festlichen Anlässen wird Maisbrei, gedämpftes Brot und gebratenes Fleisch von rituell geschlachteten Tieren in großen Eisentöpfen auf offenen Feuerstellen zubereitet.

Although the cooking done on ritual occasions tends to take place in the open, in some areas women make food in dwellings constructed for this purpose. In contrast to other spaces, the thatch is sometimes left deliberately unfinished to facilitate ventilation.

Bien que la tendance soit de cuisiner à l'extérieur lors des occasions rituelles, dans certaines régions la nourriture est préparée dans des habitations spécialement construites pour cet usage. Le toit de chaume est parfois laissé incomplet, aidant l'aération.

Das Kochen bei rituellen Anlässen wird gewöhnlich im Freien vorgenommen, aber in manchen Gebieten bereiten die Frauen das Essen auch in besonderen Hütten zu, die eigens hierfür errichtet wurden, mit einer Öffnung im Strohdach zur Ventilation.

In most homesteads people use a variety of vessels to cook and store foods, such as clay pots, and aluminium and enamel containers. Enamel has become increasingly common, but clay pots are still commonly used for brewing and consuming beer.

Dans la plupart des ménages, les gens utilisent divers pots et casseroles pour préparer les aliments, comme des pots de terre cuite et d'aluminium. Les pots émaillés sont populaires, mais ceux de terre cuite sont toujours les préférés pour la bière.

In den Heimstätten benutzt man verschiedene Töpfe zum Kochen und Lagern der Lebensmittel, darunter Ton-, Aluminium- und Emaillegefäße. Letztere sind mittlerweile sehr verbreitet, aber zum Brauen und Trinken von Bier werden weiterhin Tongefäße verwendet.

Thatch is still the preferred method of roofing homesteads, mainly because it affords excellent insulation in all seasons. Today, among some Zulu communities, aluminium sheeting is added to the bottom of the thatch to protect it from hungry goats and cows.

A cause de ses qualités isolantes en toutes saisons, le chaume est le matériau préféré pour recouvrir le toit des maisons. Dans de nombreuses communautés zouloues, on recouvre la base en aluminium, pour empêcher les chèvres et les bestiaux de le dévorer.

Reet ist weiterhin das bevorzugte Material zur Bedachung der Heimstätten, weil es zu allen Jahreszeiten gut isoliert. Manche Zulu verwenden heute zusätzlich Aluminiumblech an den Rändern, um das Strohdach vor hungrigen Ziegen und Kühen zu schützen.

Because thatch is readily available in most rural areas, it is a comparatively cheap building material. But it requires considerable maintenance and, in areas where it is prone to being struck by lightning, thatch also poses a risk to life and property.

Le chaume, qui est facile à trouver dans la plupart des régions rurales, est un matériau de construction relativement bon marché. Par contre, il exige beaucoup d'entretien, et son utilisation est risquée dans les régions orageuses.

Da Reet in den meisten ländlichen Gebieten verfügbar ist, bildet es einen preiswerten Rohstoff zum Bauen. Aber es erfordert ziemlich viel Pflege und in manchen Gegenden, wo es häufig zu Blitzschlag kommt, stellt es auch ein Risiko für Leben und Besitz dar.

Different thatching techniques are used by different South African communities: in some areas, the thatch is packed very tightly, while in others it seems quite loose and even untidy. Likewise, because thatching grass is comparatively heavy, the depth of the thatch usually varies considerably depending on the thickness of a dwelling's walls.

Les méthodes de recouvrement avec le chaume varient d'une communauté à l'autre. Dans certaines, on préfère le serrer fortement, dans d'autres, on le laisse relâché, ce qui donne un aspect désordonné. A cause de son poids, la couche de chaume dépendra de l'épaisseur des murs soutenant le toit.

Die Machart der Strohdächer ist unterschiedlich bei den verschiedenen südafrikanischen Volksgruppen: In manchen Gebieten wird das Reet fest aufgepackt, während es anderswo eher lose und fast unordentlich aussieht. Weil das Reet ziemlich schwer ist, richtet sich die Dichte der Dächer danach, wie dick die Wände der Baulichkeit sind.

Abandoned homesteads attest to the problems people face when they build using locally available materials. Unlike fired bricks, aluminium sheeting and other durable building materials, indigenous materials decay readily if left to the mercy of the elements.

Les habitations abandonnées démontrent l'infériorité des matériaux disponibles sur place. Contrairement aux matériaux solides comme les briques et la tôle d'aluminium, les matériaux indigènes se détériorent rapidement s'ils sont laissés à la merci des éléments.

Verlassene Heimstätten zeugen von der Problematik mit Rohstoffen vor Ort. Im Gegensatz zu gebrannten Ziegelsteinen, Aluminiumblech und anderen haltbaren Baumaterialien verwittern natürliche Baustoffe rasch, wenn sie den Elementen überlassen werden.

Some Zulu-speaking people still occasionally build beehive structures. In contrast to other dwellings, these structures never have windows. Open doorways are therefore the only natural source of light in the generally dim interiors of these homesteads.

De temps à autre, les Zoulous construisent encore des huttes en forme de ruche. A la différence des autres habitations, celles-ci n'ont jamais de fenêtres. La porte ouverte est donc le seul moyen d'éclairer naturellement l'intérieur plutôt sombre.

Manche Zulu errichten noch die bienenkorbförmigen Rundhütten, die im Gegensatz zu anderen Behausungen nie Fenster haben. Der offene Eingang ist daher die einzige natürliche Lichtquelle für den recht dunklen Innenraum dieser Unterkunft.

In contrast to the insulation that thatch affords throughout the year, the metal sheeting that is now used on the roofs of some dwellings not only traps the summer heat, but also fails to retain the heat generated by open fires in winter.

Le chaume est un excellent isolant en toutes saisons. Par contre, la tôle utilisée de nos jours pour recouvrir le toit de certaines habitations, non seulement retient et laisse s'accumuler la chaleur en été, mais en hiver laisse s'échapper la chaleur procurée par les feux à l'intérieur.

Im Gegensatz zu der guten Isolation, die ein Strohdach ganzjährig verschafft, leitet Wellblech, das jetzt oft zum Dachdecken benutzt wird, im Sommer die Hitze von außen in die Hütte, während es im Winter verhindert, daß sich die Wärme der offenen Feuerstelle innen speichern kann.

Although some Zulu traditionalists still build beehive homesteads, in the belief that their ancestors are unable to recognize other types of dwellings, today most Zulu families live in circular homes like those found elsewhere in South Africa. Alternatively, they build rectangular dwellings similar to those first introduced by white settlers in the 19th century.

Bien que certains traditionalistes zoulous construisent toujours des huttes en forme de ruche dans la croyance que leurs ancêtres sont incapables de reconnaître d'autres habitations, de nos jours la plupart des familles zouloues vivent dans des maisons circulaires comme partout ailleurs en Afrique du Sud. Sinon ils construisent des maisons rectangulaires semblables à celles introduites par les pionniers blancs au 19ième.

Manche Traditionalisten unter den Zulu bauen noch immer die bienenkorbförmigen Wohnhütten, weil sie glauben, daß die Ahnen andere Behausungen nicht erkennen können, aber die Mehrheit der Familien lebt mittlerweile in den Rundhütten, wie man sie überall in Südafrika antrifft. Andernfalls errichten sie rechteckige Häuser, wie sie von weißen Siedlern im 19. Jahrhundert eingeführt wurden.

Men commonly spend time separately from women in the shade cast by the homestead walls at different times of day. Alternatively, they congregate under trees for important council meetings, thus ensuring the privacy of their deliberations.

Les hommes ont tendance à se réunir entre eux, par exemple à l'ombre des murs de leurs habitations. Sinon, ils se rassemblent à l'écart sous les arbres pour d'importantes réunions du conseil, garantissant ainsi le secret de leurs délibérations.

Männer kommen meistens zusammen, ohne daß Frauen dabei sind. Sie treffen sich etwa im Schatten der Wände bei den Heimstätten, oder sie versammeln sich für wichtige Beratungen unter Bäumen, damit ihre Gespräche nicht belauscht werden können.

The materials used to construct animal enclosures vary considerably from one area to another. Where stone is readily available, it is used in preference to other, less durable materials like brushwood and the branches of thorny acacia trees.

Les matériaux utilisés pour la construction des enclos d'animaux varient d'une région à l'autre. Là où les pierres sont abondantes, elles sont choisies de préférence aux matériaux moins durables, comme les broussailles ou les branches épineuses de l'acacia.

Baumaterial für die Einfriedung von Viehgehegen unterscheidet sich von Gebiet zu Gebiet. Wo Steine zur Verfügung stehen, bevorzugt man diese gegenüber anderen, weniger haltbaren Rohstoffen wie Gehölz und dornigen Akazienzweigen.

Rural homesteads are often populated by animals like cows, goats, donkeys and chickens (*see also* page 85). Cattle and goats are slaughtered mainly on ritual occasions, their milk playing an important role in supplementing the protein needs of families living in out-lying areas. Even today, very few people in these areas have access to cars. Donkeys are therefore commonly used to transport people to and from festivals and rural markets.

Les propriétés rurales sont souvent peuplées d'animaux domestiques: chèvres, vaches, ânes et poulets (*voir aussi* page 85). Les bovidés et les chèvres sont sacrifiés lors des occasions rituelles et leur lait fournissent une majeure partie des protéines nécessaires aux familles vivant dans les régions retirées. Même de nos jours, très peu ont accès à une auto, et les ânes sont le moyen de transport normalement utilisé par la population pour se déplacer.

Anwesen auf dem Lande sind oft mit Kühen, Ziegen, Eseln und Hühnern bevölkert (*siehe auch Seite 85*). Geschlachtet werden Kühe und Ziegen hauptsächlich zu rituellen Anlässen, aber die Milch der Tiere bildet wie die Hühner einen wichtigen Bestandteil der Eiweißzufuhr bei der Ernährung. Selbst heutzutage haben nur wenige Leute in diesen Gebieten ein Auto. So ist die Eselskarre das gebräuchliche Beförderungsmittel, um die Menschen zu Festlichkeiten oder Märkten zu bringen.

Chickens and other domestic fowls like turkeys are usually allowed to roam freely in and around the homestead. Most live on the scraps of porridge and vegetable cuttings women discard before and after cooking meals for their families. Although generally no-one seems to take notice of them, women always know exactly how many chickens they own, and whether or not they lay eggs regularly.

Les poulets et autres volailles domestiques comme les dindons, vont et viennent librement dans, et autour des habitations. Ils se nourrissent des restants de porridge et légumes dont se débarrassent les femmes lors de la préparation des repas pour la famille. Bien que personne ne semble s'en occuper, les femmes savent toujours exactement combien de poules elles possèdent et si elles pondent régulièrement ou non.

Hühner und anderes Geflügel wie Puten laufen bei den Heimstätten meist frei herum und ernähren sich von Breiklecksen und Gemüseabfall, wie sie bei der Zubereitung der Mahlzeiten anfallen. Obwohl sich niemand darum zu kümmern scheint, wissen die Frauen immer ganz genau, wie viele Hühner ihnen gehören und ob diese regelmäßig Eier legen.

Since they do not have access to expensive commercially manufactured toys, children in rural communities entertain themselves in a variety of ways. Some have dogs as pets, while others play with wheelbarrows and cooking pots. It is also common for children from these communities to make their own toys from sun-baked clay and materials like wire, which is commonly used to fence fields and other enclosures.

N'ayant pas accès aux jouets, souvent hors de prix, vendus dans le commerce, les enfants des communautés rurales doivent s'amuser à leur façon. Certains ont des chiens, d'autres jouent avec des brouettes et des ustensiles de cuisine. Ces enfants fabriquent souvent leurs jouets eux-mêmes, avec de la glaise séchée au soleil et du fil de clôture qui est facile à trouver.

Da ihnen keine teuren Spielsachen zur Verfügung stehen, vergnügen sich die Kinder auf dem Lande auf alle mögliche Art und Weise. Manche haben einen Hund als Haustier, andere spielen mit Schubkarren und Kochtöpfen. Hier fertigen sich die Kinder auch häufig ihr Spielzeug selbst an, etwa aus sonnengetrocknetem Lehm oder aus Draht, wie er für die Einzäunung von Feldern und Viehgehegen benutzt wird.

Ndebele people sometimes add elaborate façades to homesteads and important communal spaces like churches. The shapes of these façades are often echoed in court-yard walls, reinforcing the gran-deur of these buildings. But rural communities are not necessarily concerned with preserving these comparatively unusual architec-tural features once buildings of this kind have been abandoned.

Les Ndebeles ajoutent parfois des ornements à la façade de leurs habitations et de certaines con-structions importantes comme les églises. Le style de ces façades se retrouve aussi souvent dans les murs de la propriété, accentuant l'éminence de ces édifices. Toute-fois, la communauté ne se soucie pas toujours de préserver ces ex-térieurs distinctifs une fois que ces constructions ont été abandonnées.

Die Ndebele versehen die eigene Heimstätte und wichtige gemein-schaftliche Gebäude wie Kirchen oft mit kunstvollen Fassaden. Die Form dieser Fassaden wird dann häufig an den Wänden der Innen-höfe wiederholt, wodurch diese Baulichkeiten ein imposanteres Aussehen erhalten. Aber die Land-bevölkerung zeigt kein Interesse, diese recht ungewöhnlichen Bau-merkmale zu erhalten, wenn Ge-bäude nicht mehr genutzt werden.

Homesteads may be abandoned once their inhabitants die or move to new sites, in search of better fields for planting maize and other produce, or in the hope of finding grazing. As it is believed that a family's ancestors continue to occupy these sites, others generally refrain from vandalising them. Homesteads are left to decay naturally, slowly eroding during the annual rainy season.

Les habitations pourront être abandonnées en cas de décès, ou si les occupants partent à la recherche de terres meilleures pour cultiver le maïs et autres produits agricoles, ou dans l'espoir de trouver plus d'herbages. La croyance veut que les ancêtres de la famille continuent à occuper l'endroit, le protégeant donc contre le vandalisme. Les habitations sont laissées aux éléments qui les éroderont petit à petit au cours des saisons.

Wenn die Besitzer sterben oder abwandern, gewöhnlich auf der Suche nach besserem Ackerboden zum Anpflanzen von Mais oder anderen Produkten oder in der Hoffnung, zusätzliches Weideland zu finden, werden die Heimstätten dem Verfall preisgegeben. Weil der Glaube besteht, daß die Ahnen der Familie weiterhin dort anwesend sind, trauen sich andere nicht, diese Stätten zu beschädigen. So verwittern Heimstätten auf natürliche Art, indem sie sich im Regen langsam auflösen.

In contemporary rural homesteads the past often meets the present. Women continue to produce the mural designs and techniques they learn from their mothers, but they also use plastic containers and other commercially manufactured vessels rather than clay pots.

Dans les habitations rurales, le passé souvent rencontre le présent. Les femmes continuent de décorer les murs suivant les techniques apprises de leurs mères, mais elles préfèrent les seaux et récipients en plastique plutôt que les pots en terre cuite.

In ländlichen Gebieten treffen sich oftmals Vergangenheit und Zukunft. Frauen fertigen immer noch Wandmalereien an, wie ihre Mütter es sie gelehrt haben, aber sie benutzen auch Plastikbehälter und andere Gefäße aus dem Handel anstelle von Tontöpfen.